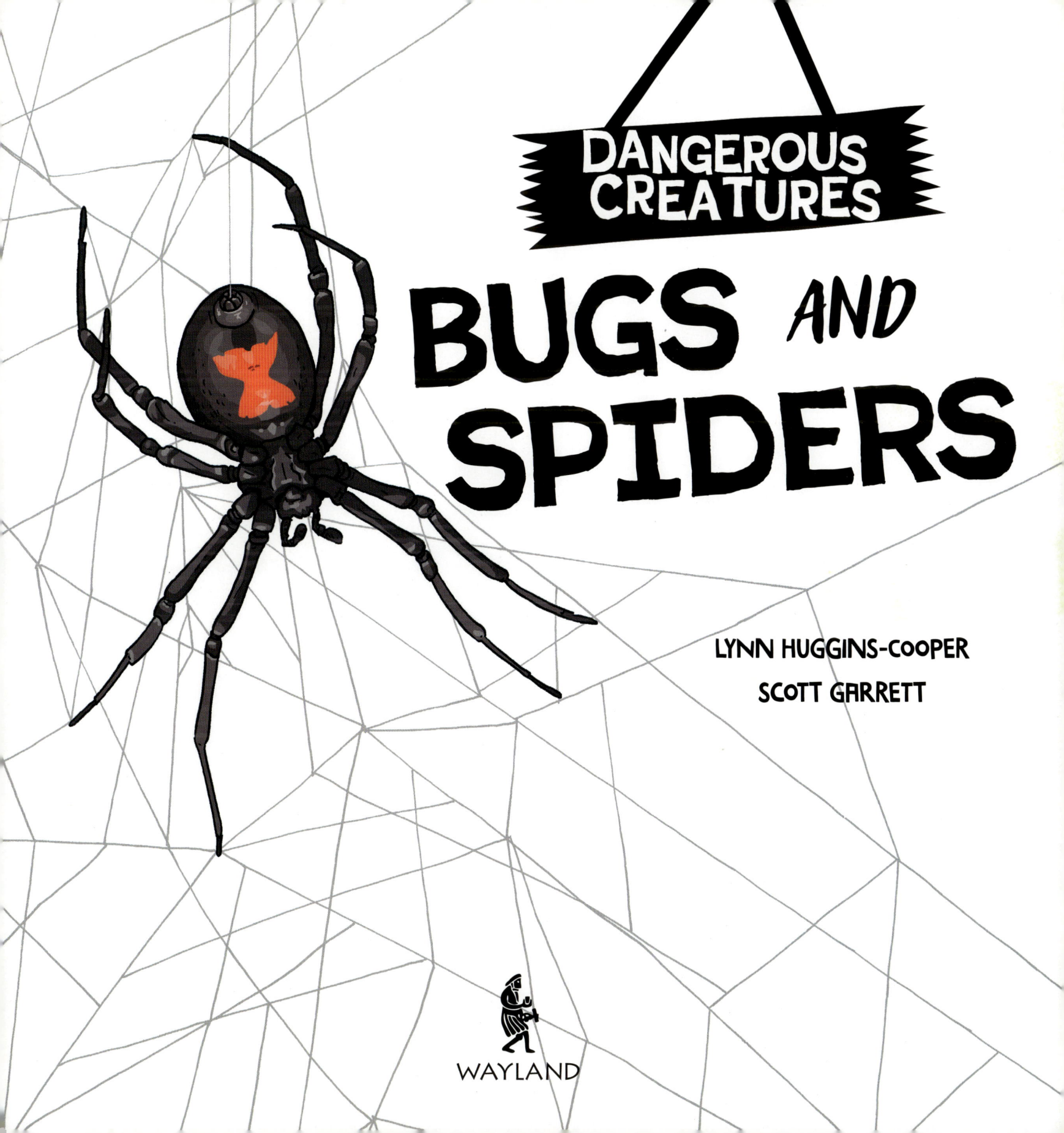

# DANGEROUS CREATURES

# BUGS AND SPIDERS

LYNN HUGGINS-COOPER
SCOTT GARRETT

WAYLAND

First published in Great Britain in 2025
by Wayland
Copyright © Hodder and Stoughton, 2025
All rights reserved

Commissioning editor: Jenni Lazell
Design manager: Lisa Peacock

HB ISBN: 978 1 5263 2837 3
PB ISBN: 978 1 5263 2838 0

Printed and bound in Dubai
Wayland, an imprint of Hachette
Children's Group
Part of Hodder and Stoughton
Carmelite House
50 Victoria Embankment
London EC4Y 0DZ

An Hachette UK Company
www.hachette.co.uk
www.hachettechildrens.co.uk

The website addresses (URLs) included in this book were valid at the time of going to press. However, it is possible that contents or addresses may have changed since the publication of this book. No responsibility for any such changes can be accepted by either the author or the Publisher.

The authorised representative in the EEA is Hachette Ireland, 8 Castlecourt Centre, Dublin 15, D15 XTP3, Ireland
(email: info@hbgi.ie)

# CONTENTS

BEASTLY BUGS AND SAVAGE SPIDERS 4

FIRE ANTS 6

MOSQUITOES 8

SIX-EYED SAND SPIDERS 10

FLANNEL MOTH CATERPILLARS 12

BLACK WIDOW SPIDERS 14

CREEPY CRAWLY TACTICS 16

PRAYING MANTIS 18

KILLER BEES 20

BROWN RECLUSE SPIDERS 22

ASSASSIN BUGS 24

GOLIATH BIRD-EATING TARANTULAS 26

DANGEROUS CREATURE FACTS 28

GLOSSARY 30

FIND OUT MORE 31

INDEX 32

# BEASTLY BUGS AND SAVAGE SPIDERS

Insects and other creepy crawlies may look small and harmless, and lots of them are, feasting on leaves and pretty flowers. But some are absolutely ruthless and can cause nasty damage ... to other insects. Read on to find out more about these miniature predators.

## SIMILAR ... BUT DIFFERENT

Bugs and spiders are both invertebrates, which means they don't have backbones. Instead they have an exoskeleton, a hard, protective outer coating which protects their bodies. There are a few features that make them unique from each other, though.

Extra legs – no fair!

Cool wings.

# MINIBEAST ANATOMY

All insects have six legs, wings and a body made up of three parts.

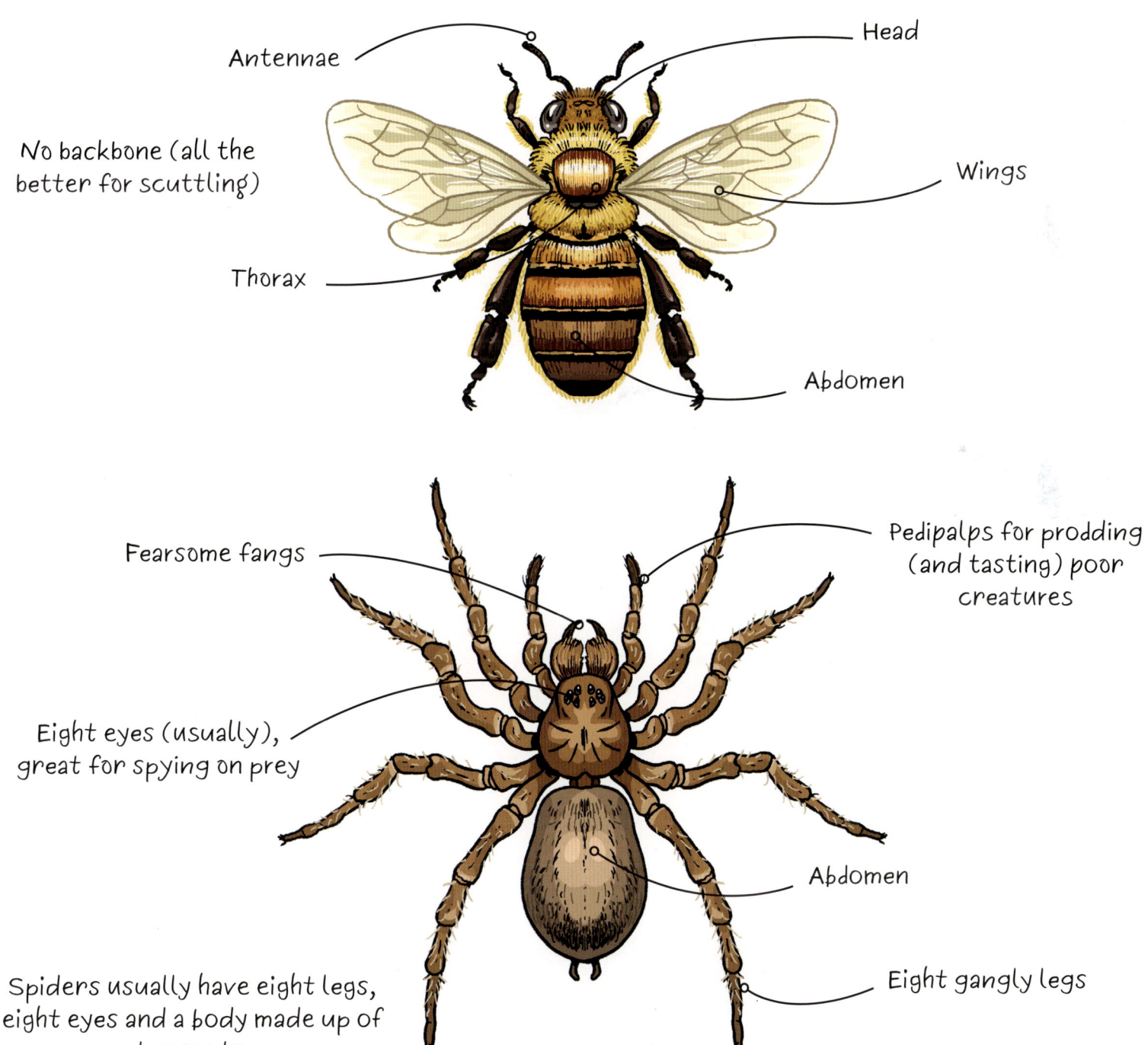

- Antennae
- Head
- No backbone (all the better for scuttling)
- Wings
- Thorax
- Abdomen

- Fearsome fangs
- Pedipalps for prodding (and tasting) poor creatures
- Eight eyes (usually), great for spying on prey
- Abdomen
- Eight gangly legs

Spiders usually have eight legs, eight eyes and a body made up of two parts.

# FIRE ANTS

Fire ants originally come from South America. Now they are found across the world in warm and tropical places, such as parts of the USA, Africa and Asia. They are small but mighty, and rely on teamwork to attack their victims.

Fire ants live in dome-shaped soil mounds that can be up to 30 cm high. Worker ants dig the tunnels while queen ants lay the eggs.

Fire ants eat carrion (dead animals), insects and small animals. They have even been known to attack young horses and calves that are too small to run away.

They kill by hanging on with their sharp jaws, as they use their stingers to inject venom into their prey.

All hands on deck!

Not only are fire ants strong, carrying up to 20 times their own body weight, but they can also cross water and survive floods by joining together in clumps and creating a floating raft.

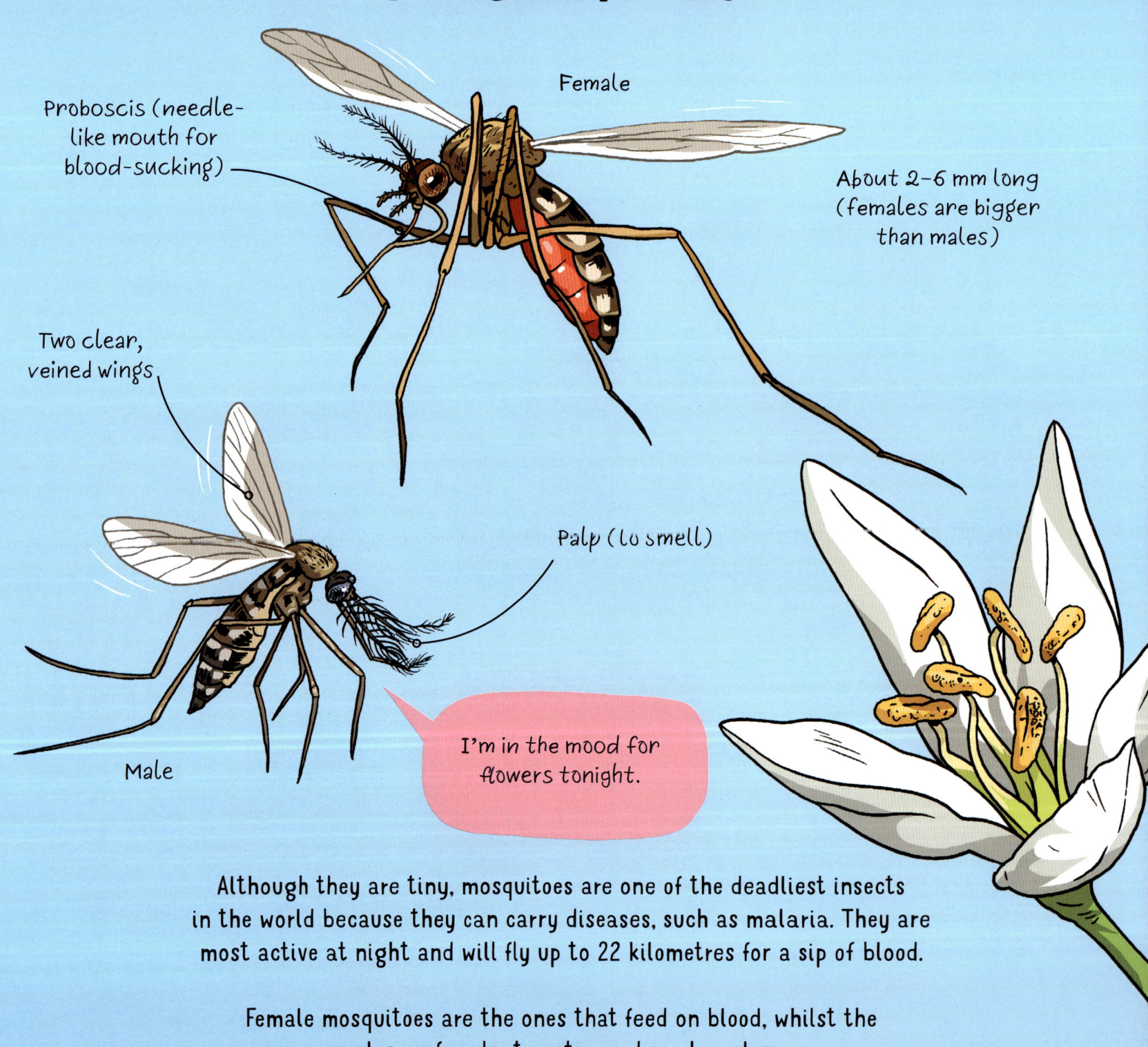

Although they are tiny, mosquitoes are one of the deadliest insects in the world because they can carry diseases, such as malaria. They are most active at night and will fly up to 22 kilometres for a sip of blood.

Female mosquitoes are the ones that feed on blood, whilst the males prefer plant nectar and are harmless.

These bloodthirsty beasts find their victims by sensing the carbon dioxide gas that animals – including humans – breathe out. Mosquitoes use their strong proboscis to pierce flesh and suck blood.

EEEEEEEEEEEEEEEEEE

EEEEEEEEEEEEEEEEEE

Our immune system is actually what makes mosquito bites itch, as our bodies react to the proteins that the mosquito injects to help it suck out blood.

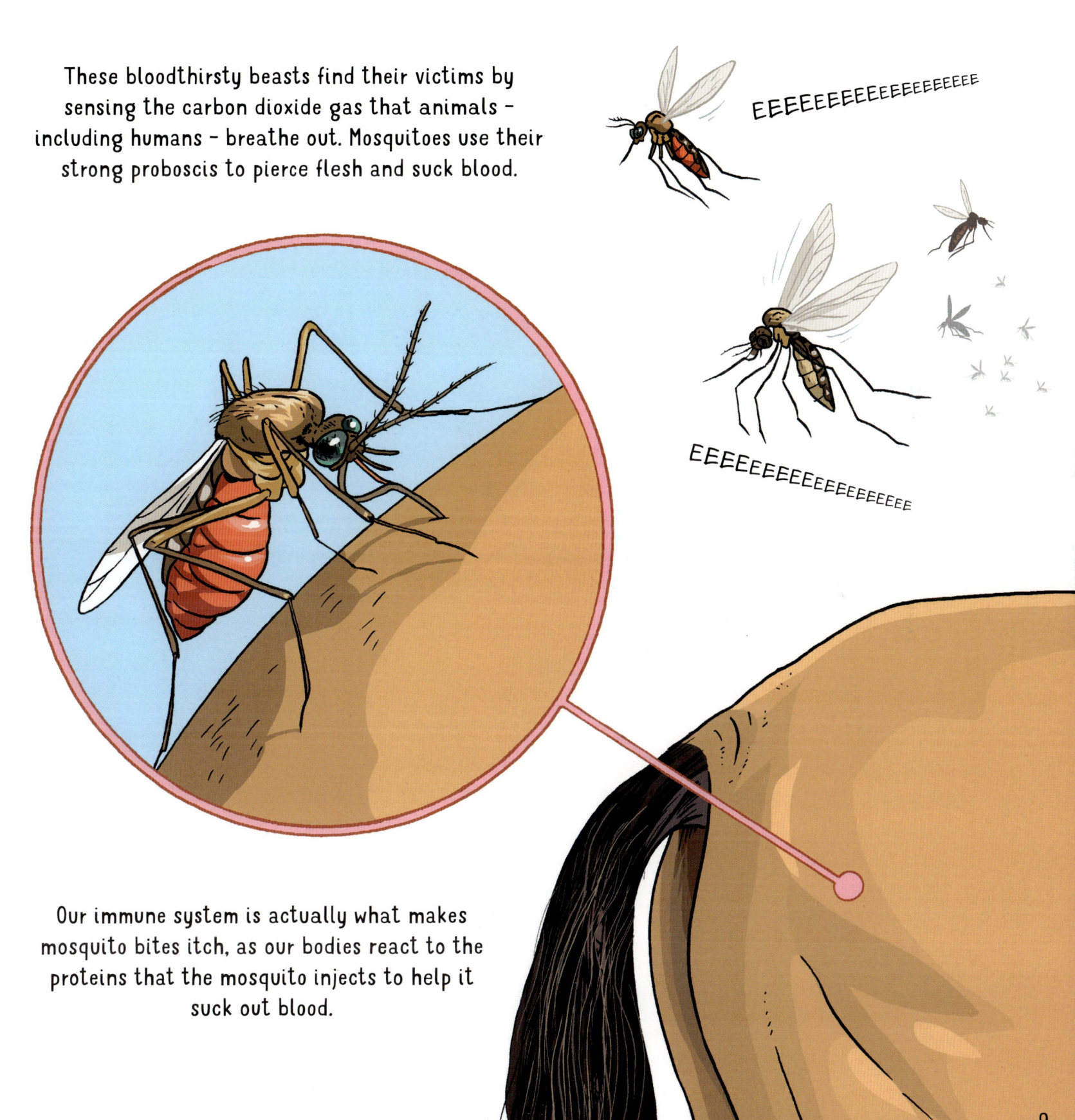

# SIX-EYED SAND SPIDERS

Body 0.9–1.9 cm long with legs as long as 5 cm

Six eyes, rather than eight (like most spiders)

Their legs look a lot like a crab's legs

Six-eyed sand spiders, also known as six-eyed crab spiders, have lived on Earth for millions of years. They are found in southwest Africa, usually in deserts and dry areas, buried in sand dunes or under rocks.

Six-eyed sand spiders are sly killers. They scoop out sand to make a pit, crawl into the pit and cover themselves with sand. And then they wait ...

As the prey walks across the pit, the spider leaps up and grabs the insect with its front legs.

The venom from a sand spider can cause bleeding inside the body. But luckily for humans, these critters live in remote deserts, so it's very rare to come across one in daily life.

# FLANNEL MOTH CATERPILLARS

Fluffy looking, a bit like a cotton ball

Short, venomous hollow spikes under the hairs

Head and legs not visible from above

I may look soft, but I WILL damage you.

Up to 3.6 cm long

These fluffy-looking creepy crawlies are found in parts of the USA — Texas, Maryland, Florida and Missouri, and in Mexico. They are herbivores and feed on the leaves of elm, oak, plum, rose, wild cherry, holly and sycamore trees. In Mexico they are known as 'el perrito' (little dog). Harmless, right?

They use their poisonous spikes to protect themselves rather than to attack other animals. They have short, hollow spikes under their hairs that, if touched, can break off and release venom. Flannel moth caterpillars can sting even when they are dead. Best to avoid them!

Hey, I'm still scary!

After 5-6 weeks, flannel moth caterpillars turn into flannel moths. They don't build cocoons like other caterpillars, but instead change into moths inside their own skin during winter. It can look like they are dead, but in spring they break out of their old skin, ready for their big reveal as a totally harmless adult moth.

# BLACK WIDOW SPIDERS

Venom is contained inside their abdomen

Red 'hourglass' mark on the female's abdomen is only visible from below

About 2-2.5 cm long (males are half the size of females)

Black widow spiders are found in warm, tropical regions. They also live in the deserts of southwestern USA. They get their name from the practice of females devouring the male after mating.

They build their webs close to the ground, in log piles, under stones or in the burrows of small animals. Their webs can be as wide as 30 cm. If you disturb one of these spiders, it could give you a nasty bite.

Male black widows are harmless but the females are poisonous. They are shy and hide in their webs during the day.

At night, they hang belly-up in the middle of their webs. They wait for insects and small reptiles to be caught in the web.

The spiders inject their trapped prey with venom and digestive juices which stops the prey from moving and eventually kills it. The victim's flesh then becomes mushy enough for the spider to slurp up, yum!

Wait! I don't want to be a smoothie!

# CREEPY CRAWLY TACTICS

Minibeasts are small but deadly, that's for sure! But how do minibeasts manage to capture their unsuspecting victims? Check out these cunning (and freaky) killer tricks.

## MIMICRY

The orchid mantis has an amazing ability to blend into its flowery surroundings, even swaying in the breeze, as if it were a plant. It lies in wait for fruit flies and other small insects but will also lash out if it feels threatened. Sensitive soul!

Sharp teeth

Looks like orchid or papaya tree flowers

Up to 5 cm long

*Don't stop! I'm still hungry.*

## TEAM EFFORT

Many ant species, including these army ants, work together to capture prey. They are always on the move and have a giant appetite, eating large parts of the forest floor and any unlucky insects that get in their way.

Two pairs of wings

Eyes with 360 degree views

Up to 8 cm long

## SPEED

Dragonflies are harmless to humans, but in the insect world they are ruthless, catching up to 95% of their prey. They have 360 degree vision, meaning that they can see everything around them. They hunt most of their victims in mid-air and will eat them as they fly, at speeds of up to 54 km per hour.

## AMBUSH

Trapdoor spiders don't wait for their visitors to knock ... They have special teeth used to dig tube-like burrows with a hinged lid that looks like a plug. When they hear prey passing, they push the door open and grab them!

Surprise!

## DEADLY AIM

Spitting spiders spit out a sticky venomous web that stuns their prey from a short distance. This gives the spider enough time to approach and deliver a nasty bite! What's more impressive is that these spiders can even hit their targets in the dark.

# PRAYING MANTIS

- Body shape gets mistaken for a leaf
- Two large eyes and three smaller eyes
- Triangular head that can turn 180 degrees (half a circle)
- Strong jaws
- 15-12 cm long
- Praying for dinner
- Folded wings
- 'Ear-like' organ in their chest for superb hearing

The praying mantis gets its name from the way its front legs are folded in a prayer-like position, as it waits patiently to catch a snack. Praying mantises can be found all over the world, but they tend to live in warmer climates among grasslands or tropical plants that they can blend into.

The praying mantis stalks or ambushes its prey.
When ready, its front legs spring out and grip onto its victim.
The legs are lined with sharp spines, like a claw.

It's been fun, but ... it's time to bite your head off.

The praying mantis' diet includes frogs, lizards, newts and even mice. But quite strangely, they are also known to eat each other! After mating, the female mantis bites into her male partner's head as if it were a juicy piece of fruit.
Brains for breakfast, anyone?

# KILLER BEES

2 cm long (smaller than European honey bees)

Wings

Mandibles for grabbing and biting food (but also for grooming once dinner time is over)

Pollen basket

Only the female worker bees have a poisonous stinger

Africanised, or killer, honey bees came from a disastrous experiment to make more honey. African honey bees were taken to Brazil and bred with European bees. But they became much more aggressive in the process. They soon escaped and spread very quickly across the USA.

They do make mighty delicious honey, though. How can a creature so deadly create something so sweet?!

# BROWN RECLUSE SPIDERS

Body about 1 cm long

Violin-shaped mark on its head

Can be light brown, dark brown or grey

Six eyes rather than eight, like most spiders

Males have a smaller body than females but longer legs

Brown recluses are found in central and southern parts of the USA. They are called recluse spiders because they are shy and like to hide in dark places. They are also known as fiddleback or violin spiders because of the violin-shaped mark on their heads.

They can go for five months without any food or water. But if they encounter another recluse they won't pass up the chance to eat them (they're cannibals).

Brown recluses are nocturnal. During the day they sleep in their messy webs. But at night, they look for food. Male recluse spiders are scavengers and eat carrion (dead animals). The females are the ones who attack bugs with their fangs and inject venom.

Recluses only bite people when they are disturbed, for example if someone accidentally touches them or their web, and although their venom is deadlier than some snakes, the amount of venom they inject is too small to cause serious damage to humans.

# ASSASSIN BUGS

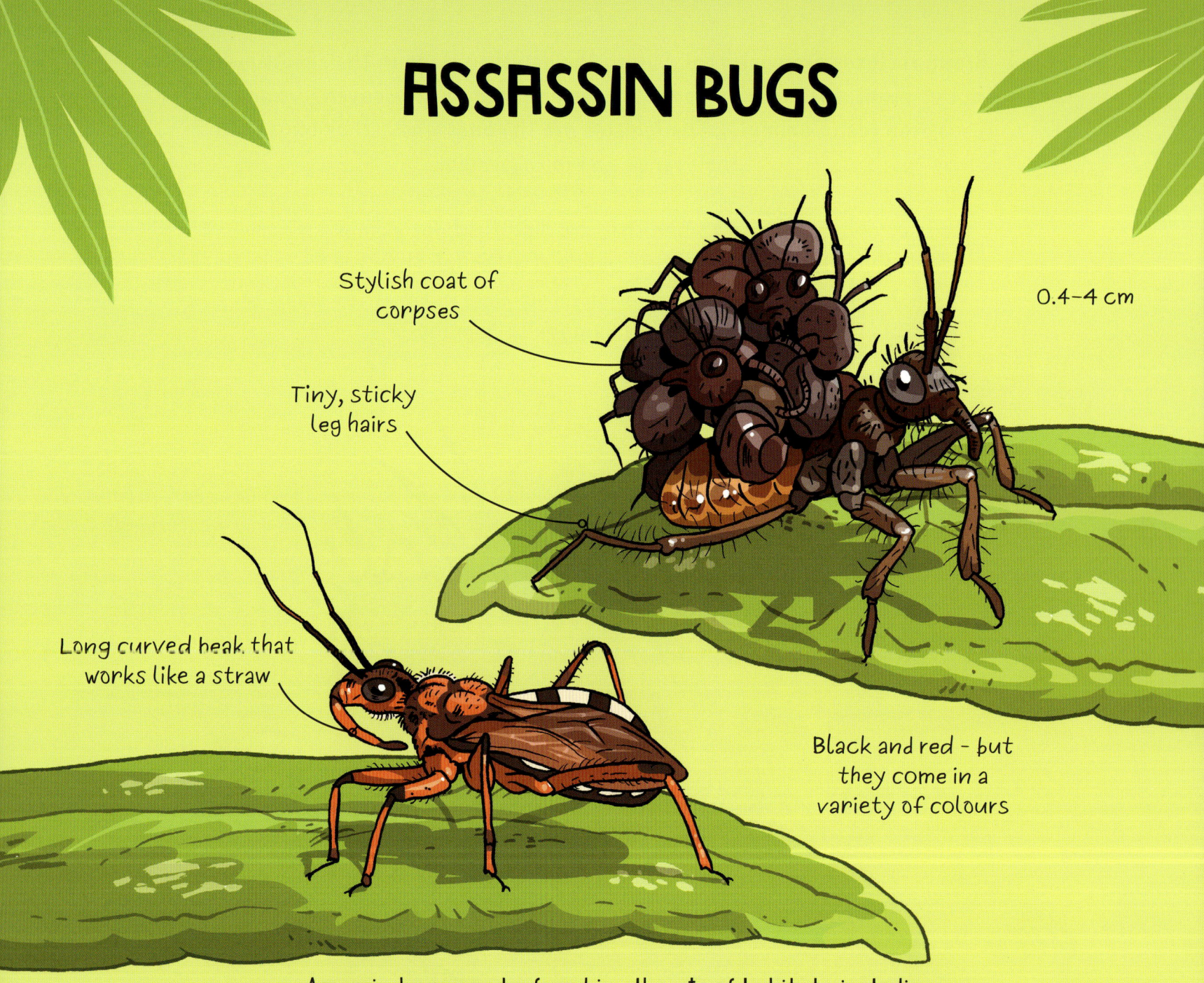

Stylish coat of corpses

Tiny, sticky leg hairs

0.4–4 cm

Long curved beak that works like a straw

Black and red – but they come in a variety of colours

Assassin bugs can be found in all sorts of habitats including rainforests and rocky landscapes. The majority live in North America.

Assassin bugs can camouflage themselves either as a ball of dust, or in some cases with the dead bodies of other insects, such as flies and ants. This is a smart way to avoid becoming someone else's dinner. It looks scary and the scent means that other bugs have no idea who's behind the mask!

# GOLIATH BIRD-EATING TARANTULAS

Body up to 12 cm long

Eight eyes

Fangs

Two 'pedipalps' for moving prey

30-cm-long legs for creeping around

Hairs on the legs sense movement from other creatures

These huge spiders are creatures from nightmares and horror films, with their hairy bodies and long, wiry legs. The Goliath bird-eater is the biggest of them all, found living under rocks and plant roots in the rainforests of northern South America.

Despite their name, they rarely eat birds. Instead they dine on insects as well as rodents, bats and lizards – whatever comes along!

# DANGEROUS CREATURE FACTS

### LARGEST
The Goliath bird-eating tarantula certainly wins the trophy for the largest spider. It can also live for up to 20 years. Now that's impressive!

### BEST DISGUISE
The orchid mantis gets the award for the prettiest killer, confusing its victims by lurking among gorgeous plants.

### FASTEST BITE
The Dracula ant snaps its jaws incredibly fast. This can either kill or stun its victim. Scientists say the Dracula ant's jaws close 5,000 times quicker than the blink of an eye.

## TOP 5 DEADLIEST* BUGS AND SPIDERS

1. MOSQUITO
2. ASSASSIN BUG
3. AFRICANISED HONEY BEE
4. BLACK WIDOW SPIDER
5. BROWN RECLUSE SPIDER

* causing most harm to humans

That daddy long legs dangling by the window doesn't seem too threatening now, huh?

*I'm full of poison, I just haven't figured out how to use it ...*

*I'd like to thank all the sleeping beauties out there.*

### DEADLIEST

Certain types of mosquito spread diseases like malaria and yellow fever, killing more people each year than any other creature in the world. Medical experts continue to find new treatments for diseases spread by mosquitoes and, of course, it's important to know that not all mosquitoes are deadly.

### MOST TOXIC

Harvester ants have the most toxic and powerful venom of any insect on the planet. Twelve stings from an itsy bitsy harvester ant is enough to kill a 2 kg rat!

### BEST AT HIDING

Bugs and spiders are all pretty good at hiding, but the six-eyed sand spider surely wins the medal. It must be lurking here somewhere!

# GLOSSARY

**Abdomen**
The lower part of a spider's body.

**Ambush**
A surprise attack from a hidden place.

**Burrow**
A hole dug by an animal.

**Camouflage**
The special colours or markings found on plants and animals that help them to remain hidden.

**Carnivores**
Animals that eat only meat.

**Endangered species**
A group of living things in danger of dying out completely.

**Fangs**
A spider's long hollow teeth. Spiders use their fangs to inject deadly venom and to attack their prey.

**Funnel-shaped**
A tube that starts out wide and becomes more narrow, for example, an ice-cream cone.

**Hourglass**
An instrument that measures time using sand in a vase-like container.

**Livestock**
Animals, such as cows and sheep, that are farmed by people.

**Mimicry**
To copy or imitate something else to confuse other animals and avoid being eaten or to capture prey.

**Pedipalps**
Two long limbs (a bit like arms) on the front of a spider's head, used for feeling and holding things in place.

**Pollinator**
An animal or insect that helps transport pollen from one flower to another and helps plants to reproduce.

**Predators**
Animals that hunt other animals.

**Prey**
Animals hunted by other animals for food.

**Proboscis**
A thin, tube-like mouth part on insects.

# FIND OUT MORE

**Check out these books and websites to become an expert on bugs and spiders.**

Read *Bugs Save the World* by Buglife: the Invertebrate Conservation Trust (Wayland, 2022) to find out why bugs are so important – to humans, animals and the survival of our planet.

Did you know up to 10 quintillion insects are crawling around the world, but only just over a million species have been named? Read *One Million Insects* by Isabel Thomas (Welbeck, 2021) to find out more.

What even is entomology? Read *Science-ology: Entomology* (Wayland, 2023) to explore the science of insects.

Need help identifying an insect? Visit this site for a handy guide.
*www.royensoc.co.uk/understanding-insects*

Watch how the trapdoor spider catches a meal.
*www.youtube.com/watch?v=6ui0hbv3wVs*

Mantis vs jumping spider? See it here:
*www.youtube.com/watch?v=7wKu13wmHog*

# INDEX

Africanised honey bees 20–21, 29
ambush 11, 17, 19
antennae 5
ants 6–7, 16, 28, 29
army ants 16
assassin bugs 24–25, 29

bees 20–21, 29
black widow spiders 14–15, 29
blood suckers 8, 9
body parts 5
brown recluse spiders 22–23, 29

camouflage 16, 18, 24, 28
cannibals 19, 22
carrion 7, 23
caterpillars 12–13

daddy long legs 29
diseases 8, 29
Dracula ants 28
dragonflies 17

exoskeletons 4

fangs 5, 23, 26, 27
fire ants 6–7
flannel moth caterpillars 12–13
frogs 27

Goliath bird-eating tarantulas 26–27, 28

harvester ants 29

invertebrates 4

jaws 6, 7, 18, 28

killer bees 20–21

malaria 8, 29
mandibles 20
mantises 16, 18–19, 28
mimicry 16
mosquitoes 8–9, 29
moths 13

nocturnal creatures 23

orchid mantises 16, 28

pedipalps 5, 26
praying mantises 18–19
proboscis 8, 9

scavengers 7, 23
six-eyed sand spiders 10–11, 29
spiders 4, 5, 10–11, 14–15, 17, 22–23, 25, 26–27, 28, 29
spikes 12, 13
spitting spiders 17
stings 6, 7, 13, 20, 21, 29
swarms 21

teamwork 6, 7, 16, 21
trapdoor spiders 17

venom 7, 11, 13, 14, 15, 17, 23, 27, 29
violin spiders *see* brown recluse spiders

webs 14, 15, 17, 23, 25
wings 5, 8, 17, 18